Conspiracy Rhetoric

Thomas Adamo

A Woodbine Cottage Publication

A Woodbine Cottage Publication
PO Box 211
Lakehurst, NJ 08733-0211
awcpublications@aol.com

Copyright 2010 by Thomas Adamo

ISBN: 1-4505-7431-9
EAN-13:   978-1-4505-7431-0

Thomas Adamo is a professor of speech and rhetoric. His areas of study and research include communication theory, political philosophy, history, and media studies.

Conspiracy Rhetoric

1. <u>INTRODUCTION</u>

The purpose of this investigation is a brief evaluation of the growing persuasive appeal of conspiracy theories within mainstream American society. The examination of this phenomenon as a contemporary social narrative will proceed through a content analysis of its public literature in order to determine what common links connect the various expressions of this cultural genre, and how its existence reflects on the larger culture. To accomplish this, a literature review will reflect on pertinent contemporary studies, and a methodology of rhetorical analysis based on classical paradigms will examine a case study of this rhetorical form.

As conspiracy theories have become a more prominent and mainstream form of cultural discourse, it will become increasingly necessary to evaluate these narratives to determine how they reflect the anxieties of the broader culture. Professor Joli Jenson clarified the challenge and goal of this type of research:

> Social narratives are convincing because they engage and confirm the taken-for-granted assumptions about the world. This means they are particularly hard to analyze, refute, or surpass. But if we can temporarily suspend ... belief in a particular social narrative and examine its central terms and logic, we can at least partially question its usefulness. ... [We must] locate and clarify the fundamental assumptions that operate in this terrain, in order to make them available for reassessment. (Jensen, 13-14)

In addition to examining the problem of why individuals and groups adhere to conspiratorial beliefs, this will address several sub-problems. The historical background of conspiracy theories will provide a context for the contemporary infatuation with them. Different types of conspiracy theories will also help determine similarities and differences among these various narratives in order to determine if there is an overall cohesion, which defines "conspiracy theory" as a concept. Moreover, these interrelations will demonstrate that theorists will be more likely to cite other conspiracy theories, and "untestable suppositions and abstract principles," as evidence to support their positions, than to depend on independent sources for confirmation (Goertzel, 741). Finally, the presentation of conspiracy theories in technology and popular culture will help determine how these instruments have assisted in the diffusion of the idea of conspiracy.

The United States has historically been fertile ground for conspiracy stories of all types, but as certain elements of society have begun to take these forms of communication seriously enough to act of them, the Oklahoma City bombing being the most prominent and tragic example, it is becoming increasingly necessary to understand this particular type of social narrative. If conspiracy theories were primarily the domain of a radical counterculture, then an analysis would not prove to be as challenging since these theories would be located in specific, easily identifiable segments of society. However, the past decade has witnessed an explosion of belief, by the general population, in a variety of conspiracy theories.

These ideas diffuse rapidly through the media of modern technology, especially the Internet and various entertainment outlets. As these messages gain increased reception by the public, there is a very great likelihood that they will begin to permeate the *Weltanschauung* that is the fundamental world-view of average Americans. Considering the violence that this type of thinking has caused recently, and historically, the growing acceptance of Conspiracism, as Pipes termed it, is a potential cause for concern. Therefore, gaining an understanding of why this particular social narrative has grown in acceptance is crucial in determining where this widespread acceptance may lead, and how to counter its negative influences.

Conspiracy theories exist in nearly every culture and they have generally mirrored social currents largely at odds with mainstream society. Their presence and prominence can serve as a barometer to chart the direction of the larger culture through the activities of this counterculture. However, without a proper understanding of the thinking preceding this type of mindset, the researcher of particular facets of this phenomenon becomes mired in a labyrinth of rhetoric that defies examination. Therefore, by gaining a broader understanding of why these theories spread, and examining the presuppositions of specific theories, conclusions concerning why specific individuals and groups adhere to them can be made.

The focus of this research is neither to prove nor disprove specific conspiracy theories, but rather to determine the rhetorical influences that operate to keep these narratives alive. Also, although it is undeniable that true conspiracies have occurred throughout history, and that these plots have been instrumental in fomenting further conspiracy theories, this study is specifically concerned with the conspiracy theory as a form of cultural communication (See Marin & Gegax, 3; Pipes, 20-1). A variety of sources will demonstrate consistencies and redundancies of specific themes concerning conspiracy.

Primary and secondary historical literature will observe the evolution of these accounts from the past to the present to demonstrate how these stories have adapted to fit contemporary milieu. The resulting narratives will very often contain a century's old tale updated with the latest new villains imbued with the power and resources to assassinate political leaders, disrupt the economy, or take over the world, depending on how vast the alleged scheme is. Upon demonstrating this historical context, an examination of contemporary manifestations of Conspiracism will show the current ideas expressed through conspiracy theories.

These pieces of literature constitute ideological narratives because, for the most part, the individuals expressing these ideas truly believe in them. Finally, Popular manifestations of Conspiracism will be examined in order to verify the types of communications related to conspiracy theories which are currently being presented to the broader public, often primarily for their entertainment value. The examinations of these latter two incarnations of literature are important because, as conspiracy theories have become a more prominent form of public discourse, there may be a symbiotic relationship observed between true ideologues and the various manifestations of public entertainment. Popular culture often uses bone-fide conspiracy theories as the bases for their communications, while ideologues use popular manifestations of Conspiracism as a supplementary basis for seeking, creating, and confirming further conspiracy theories.

When appropriate, the communication techniques employed in broader areas of persuasion and propaganda will demonstrate how these ideas spread. Despite the extensive detail used by conspiracy theorists to corroborate their claims, it may become apparent that the primary persuasive tools used by Conspiracism are fear, anxiety, and paranoia. Incredulous amounts of information are often used in the construction of various theories, but behind this facade, the conspiracy theory is primarily an emotional appeal based on the supposition of fear. This is similar to Nazi propagandist Hugo Ringler, who insisted,

It was not so much the contents of speech as it was the manner in which it was delivered that influenced the listener and won him to us. ... There are speakers who investigate and carve up their subject with almost scientific exactitude and utterly forget that they are supposed to be preaching a worldview. (Ringler, 1)

Therefore, even when contrary proof is presented, the legitimacy of conspiracy theories are not undermined for true believers, because their commitment is to a worldview, not truly inductive reasoning. For instance, the conceptions of many theorists plainly indicate that the apparent absence of conspiracy is the greatest proof of conspiracy. Likewise, this research will ultimately seek to discover whether conspiracy theories are ultimately grounded in a legitimate pursuit of truth or the propagation of a worldview.

As conspiracy theories become a more prominent feature in popular discourse, there is every reason to believe that adherence to Conspiracism will spread. As previously mentioned, this could be problematic when individuals place such faith in these narratives that they are motivated to action. The influence that conspiracy theories have over the actions of their adherents will be a primary criterion in determining the effects of Conspiracism on society as a whole.

Surprisingly, while there are many outlets to find information about the many conspiracy theories extant, a primary literature dealing with conspiracy theories as a social phenomenon is virtually nonexistent. This investigation will be important for a variety of fields that focus on human behavior, particularly the aberrant variety.

These fields would include, but would not be limited to, political science, journalism psychology, sociology, and law enforcement. Each of these academic spheres involves the study motivations and actions of human behavior.

This study will consist of five sections that will each play an important role in investigating the reason for the fascination that conspiracy theories hold for modern culture. The first section is this introduction, an effort to demonstrate the necessity and goals of this research. The second section will review the available literature on the subject and implications of conspiracy theory and culture.

The third section will propose a methodology for the analysis of conspiracy literature, with particular attention to the reactions that these pieces of literature attempt to impart to their readers. This model will seek specific connections between Ideological and Popular versions of conspiracy literature in order to demonstrate a symbiotic relationship between these two genres of Conspiracism. The fourth section will be an implementation of the research model. Finally, the fifth section will contain the analyses and conclusions formulated from the preceding sections.

2. LITERATURE REVIEW

Considering the historical frequency of Conspiracism in American culture, there are remarkably few pieces of literature devoted specifically to exploring the rhetorical forms of social narrative. The available research tends to follow three basic categories. The first studies are generally more current and examine the growing prominence of conspiracy theories in contemporary society. Although these studies do a good job of demonstrating that conspiracy is becoming a more conspicuous form of social narrative, they do not give many answers to explain why this form of social narrative has recently become more popular. Hence, the need for this investigation. The second form of literature examined the nature and content of conspiracy theories. These pieces were often small sections of larger studies originating from such diverse disciplines as the social sciences, history, and philosophy. Finally, several recent articles have made preliminary forays into the domain, which this investigation hopes to explore namely the persistence of Conspiracism as a worldview.

Conspiracy theories of nearly every shape, size, and variety have virtually exploded into the public consciousness over the past decade. This trend has become so conspicuous that it has attracted the attention of major media outlets. <u>Newsweek</u> published an article in late 1996 proclaiming, "Conspiracy paranoia is surrounding us. … Fomented on the Internet, mass-marketed by Hollywood Conspiracism has become a kind of para-religion." Citing a survey from <u>George</u> magazine, the authors went on to claim that: "The ranks of the darkly deluded may be growing … three quarters of Americans believe that "the Government is involved in conspiracy." Depending on your level of venality, that statistic can be read as either mass psychosis or a marketing opportunity" (Marin & Gegax, 1). Offering a hint as to why conspiracy theories evoke such interest, editor Robin Ramsey concurred saying, "These days we've got conspiracy theories everywhere; and about almost everything. … The difficulty – or the delight – for people like me is that buried in the stupid nonsense there is something of interest in almost all of these fields." Noting their relations to recent innovations in communications technology, he later speculated, "Maybe conspiracy theories are just the gossip of the global village." (Ramsey, 2 & 5)

While the popular examinations of the growth of Conspiracism may seem flippant at times, there has been at least one recent serious scholarly attempt to gauge the growing belief in conspiracy theories by the general public. Ted Goertzel, of Rutgers University, has conducted quantitative research attempting to measure how likely individuals are to believe in specific conspiracy theories. He defined his purpose as follows:

There has been no published information about the prevalence of belief in any of these conspiracies. Nor has anyone addressed the question of to what extent belief in conspiracies is a generalized ideological trait, that is, how likely are people who believe in one conspiracy to believe in others. Nor has there been any previous attempt to discover the psychological or sociological correlates of belief in conspiracies. (Goertzel, 732)

Although his primary conclusions were that a qualitative methodology would be more useful in discovering the interrelations between conspiracy theories, his methodology effectively demonstrated the pervasiveness and interrelationships involving contemporary beliefs in conspiracy theories.

Following focus group discussions that identified several widely held conspiracy theories, Goertzel conducted a telephone survey of 348 residents of southwestern New Jersey, presenting each with a list of ten conspiracy theories. Randomly selected respondents were from economically, racially, ethnically, and sociologically diverse sections of Burlington, Camden, and Gloucester counties. The sample was stratified and weighted in order to compensate for demographic anomalies, with a resulting margin of error of about 5.3%. Participants were asked to indicate, on a five-point scale ranging from "definitely true" to "definitely false," which theories they thought were likely to be valid. Over 93% of the respondents believed that at least one of the ten theories offered was definitely or probably true. After tabulating his results, Goertzel described his goals and findings as follows:

There is remarkably little psychological literature on belief in conspiracy theories. Graumann (1987, p. 245) observed that this is a "topic of intrinsic psychological interest that has been left to history and to the other social sciences." Historians (Groh, 1987) and sociologists (Lipset and Raab, 1970) find that conspiratorial thinking has been central to antisemetic and other authoritarian belief systems, and to many social movements in both Europe and the United States. ... Despite this historical evidence, conspiratorial thinking was not part of the authoritarianism syndrome as originally conceptualized by Adorno, et al. (1950), and has not been addressed in the subsequent research on authoritarianism or related social-psychological constructs. Given this lack of prior empirical research, our first goal was to determine to what extent there is a generalized tendency to believe in conspiracies. ... These data confirm that conspiracy theories are alive and well in contemporary American society. Most respondents are inclined to believe that several of a list of conspiracies are probably or definitely true. The tendency to believe in conspiracies is correlated with anomia, with a lack of trust in people, and with feelings of insecurity about unemployment. ... The strong correlation with the scale of Anomia indicates that belief in conspiracies is associated with

feelings of alienation and
disaffection from the system.
(Goertzel, 735, 738-9)

These conclusions strongly support the
rationale that instances of Conspiracism
relate to more generalized feelings of anxiety
and mistrust. Goertzel later went on to
discuss the theoretical implications of his
results. He concluded that most conspiracy
theories were monological in nature that is
they tended to ignore their contexts in all but
the shallowest respects. These constructs
are useful to adherents because, "they
provide an easy, automatic explanation for
any new phenomenon which might threaten
the belief system." Observing this tendency,
Goertzel concluded, "The key issue is not
the belief in a specific conspiracy, but the
logical processes which led to that belief"
(Goertzel, 740).

As previously asserted, conspiracy
theories do not embody an exercise of
concrete reasoning as much as they embody

an argument for a abstract worldview. Pipes noticed this as well, and remarked on how the study of Conspiracism stands in unmistakable contrast to the theoretical frameworks currently employed in most academic fields which, influenced by Marxism, favor pragmatism as a primary motivation for human action as opposed to ideas.

> The study of Conspiracism assumes that ideas have consequences. ... Ideas count too, and they have a power that goes beyond simply reflecting interests. Passion, faith, fear, and idealism matter. Even the most ruthless and cynical rulers – a Heinrich Himmler or a Stalin – are swayed by ideas and know their power over others. Indeed, one can go further and describe the fascist and communist experience as

efforts at living out intellectual dreams; in a sense, the totalitarian state makes the best case for the idealistic argument, for it follows rules capriciously created in one man's minds and has no necessary connection whatsoever to sociopolitical conditions. To neglect the role of the mind is to neglect one of the richest and most important of human impulses. (Pipes, 51)

Pipes is not the only contemporary researcher to propose that ideas have consequences, and in the realm of Conspiracism, the results can be potentially dire. Carl Sagan, in his final book <u>The Demon Haunted World</u> (1996), attributed conspiracy thinking to a draught of sound ideas, "the irrationality and gullibility of an under-educated public" (Spark, 1). Similarly, Elaine Showalter has described a more general theory of hysteria, or Hystories to use her terminology, as a narrative of extreme agitation or even madness across the social spectrum. In her conception, Conspiracism is merely a symptom of a larger social illness:

> In the interaction between 1990s millennial panic, new psychotherapies, religious fundamentalism, and American political paranoia, we can see the crucible of virulent hysterias in our own time. … As their syndromes evolve, they grow from microtales of individual affliction to panics fueled by rumors about medical, familial, community, or governmental conspiracy. As the panic reaches epidemic proportions, hysteria seeks out scapegoats and enemies – from unsympathetic doctors, abusive fathers, and working mothers

to devil-worshipping sadists, curious extraterrestrials, and evil governments. ... As we approach our own millennium, the epidemic of hysterical disorders, imaginary illnesses, and hypnotically induced pseudomemories that have flooded the media seem to be reaching a high-water mark. These Hystories are merging with the more generalized paranoias, religious revivals, and conspiracy theories that have always characterized American life and the apocalyptic anxieties that always accompany the end of a century. Now they are dispersing globally to infect other countries and cultures. (Showalter, 2)

Unfortunately, although Showalter's theory was fundamentally sound, several of her case studies involved social phenomena she viewed as psychosomatic but were subsequently proved to be valid physical and psychological ailments. Nevertheless, her statements provide valid support for the current purpose of demonstrating that conspiracy thinking has become a phenomenon of the general public, as opposed to fringe elements of society.

Ramsay identified several factors contributing to the apparently growing dissemination of conspiracy theories. The first was computer technology and advanced systems of communications. "There has been an increase in conspiracy theories; but it's also that those that exist are getting around much faster than they used to" (Ramsay, 4). George Johnson concurred with this in a slightly humorous fashion, commenting on Yale University president Timothy Dwight's 1798 speech before the graduating class: "In the days before the

Internet, when rumors had to make their way by boat and horseback instead of by waves and wire, it took perseverance to assemble the pieces of a really good conspiracy theory. In those days, information (not to be confused with knowledge) crept along slowly. How much easier it is in these modern times when bits zip around the globe at the speed of light" (Johnson, 1996).

Another factor identified by Ramsay was the gullibility of the general public. Citing the varieties of mass media consumed by the average citizen of the United States and England ("piffle at best"), he noted a widespread absence of analytical thinking in contemporary society. However, this does not necessarily imply that Conspiracism is the property of any single segment of society. As Davis stated, "American crusades against subversion have never been the monopoly of a single social class or ideology, but have been readily appropriated by highly diverse groups" (Davis, xv-xvi).

Finally, Ramsay referred to a number of instances since the earlier 1960s where, if actual conspiracies were not involved, government actions could be easily viewed as conspiratorial in nature (Ramsay, 4-5). As another source phrased it, "These bizarre fantasies would seem safely ridiculous if they didn't occasionally turn out to be true" (Marin & Gegax, 3). Each of these factors not only served to demonstrate the origins of popular conspiratorial thinking but also the modes through which it is transmitted.

Conspiracy theories used to be primarily involved with the domain of politics, but as Pipes noted, "What was once specific to politics has had a "domino effect" in the realm of culture. In the last year or so [1996], conspiracy thinking has been used as a narrative model by everyone from novelists to the makers of blockbuster movies" (Pipes, 18). This new prevalence has increased the need for a renewed effort to understand why people believe conspiracy theories. Moreover, given the fact that true conspiracies do to exist, the absence of a literature separating conspiratorial fantasy from reality could have devastating consequences if a true conspiracy were to camouflage itself under the vast cacophony of conspiracy theories. Bale commented on this dilemma:

> Very few notions generate as much intellectual resistance, hostility, and derision within academic circles as a belief in the historical importance or efficacy of political conspiracies. Even when this belief is expressed in a very cautious manner, limited to specific and restricted contexts, supported by reliable evidence, and hedged about with sort of qualifications, it still manages to transcend the boundaries of acceptable discourse and violate unspoken academic

taboos. … Most academic researchers clearly prefer to ignore the implications of conspiratorial politics altogether rather than deal directly with such controversial matters. A number of complex cultural and historical factors contribute to this reflexive and unwarranted reaction, but it is perhaps most often the direct result of a simple failure to distinguish between 'conspiracy theories' in the strict sense of the term, which are essentially elaborate fables even though they may well be based upon a kernel of truth, and the activities of actual clandestine and covert political groups, which are a common feature of modern politics. (Bale, 1)

Journalist and researcher Chip Berlet concurred with this assessment: "Separating real conspiracies from the fictional, non-rational, lunatic, or deliberately fabricated variety is the problem faced by serious researchers, activists, and journalists. [According to Berlet] the term conspiracy theorist refers to someone whose analysis of documents, statements, and other evidence has become uncoupled from a logical train of thought" (Berlet, 1-2). Others may argue that conspiracy theorists are not illogical, they merely voice logical arguments based on faulty premises. Nevertheless, the essential definition of a narrative as a conspiracy theory is crucial to determining fact from fantasy. Pipes described this as an almost exclusively subjective process: however, his primary example may prove the contrary. "One cannot treat Winston Churchill's warnings of the Nazi conspiracy in the 1930s on a par with Hitler's contemporous ravings about a Jewish conspiracy" (Pipes, 37-8).

As the following selections from authors of various backgrounds will demonstrate, although anxiety and fear are a common characteristic of conspiracy narratives, the focus of specific evaluation criteria are primarily determined by the views and dispositions of their authors. This can extend through an entire spectrum of inclinations from those openly sympathetic to conspiracy thinking to those who see conspiracy theorists as the lowest form of pseudo-intellectuals.

Shils viewed a great deal of the conspiracy thinking in political discourse as arising from the distinctively American movement historically known as Populism. Noting an extremely dualistic approach towards politics, he stated that they possessed an,

> …Attachment to the most public symbols, extreme "politicization" to the point of ideological possession, the

anchoring of one's soul in the sphere of ultimate politics [that] is the product of a state of mind which sees only white and black. Since all that is not white is not obviously black, it must be "really" black in the sense that it hides its blackness under a disguise. The wicked hide their wickedness under the conspirator's mask of innocence. Worry about conspiracy has been a constant feature of American life for half a century at least. It has fluctuated in its significance, most of the time remaining the obsession of obscure and uninfluential ranters, but at other times, especially in the past ten years [1956], rising in intensity and extending its range of influence. Anxiety about conspiracy brings with it a distortion of the conception of individual responsibility. The peculiar idea of moral infection in consequence of association with individuals of indelible wickedness leads to a notion of "guilt by association." Conspiracy is conceived, not necessarily as oriented towards the performance of specific acts, but as the harboring of certain general states of mind in seclusion or secrecy. The tendency to prosecute for conspiracy has been growing in American practice over the past twenty-five years, a period which coincides with an upward swing of populism. (Shils, 45)

This conception viewed Conspiracism as primarily a movement of hyper-patriotic, conservative, and rural origins, reflecting the demography of populism. Although conspiracy thinking can be located throughout the political spectrum, Shils served to demonstrate a widely held stereotype that conspiracy theories originate primarily from, as it is commonly termed, the right side of the political spectrum.

The philosopher Karl Popper expressed similar sentiments, but in the language of social science,

> In order to explain what is, I think, the central task of social science, I should like to begin by describing a theory which is held by very many rationalists – a theory which I think implies exactly the opposite of the true aim of the social sciences. I shall call this theory the 'conspiracy theory of society.' This theory, which is more primitive than most forms of

theism, is akin to Homer's theory of society. Homer conceived the power of the gods in such a way that whatever happened on the plain before Troy was only a reflection of the various conspiracies on Olympus. The conspiracy theory of society is just such a version of this theism, of a belief in gods whose whims and wills rule everything. It comes from abandoning God and then asking: "Who is in his place?" His place is then filled by various powerful men and groups – sinister pressure groups, who are to be blamed for having planned the great depression and all the evils from which we suffer. (Popper, 123)

Despite his agreement with Shils, in terms of attitude, Popper did not locate the theorists of conspiracy within the activists of populism, but rather in the presumably scientific movement of rationalism. He later went on to state his own theory as to why Conspiracism is untenable as a worldview:

> Against the conspiracy theory of society I do not, of course, assert that conspiracies never happen. But I assert two things. First, they are not very frequent, and do not change the character of social life. Assuming that conspiracies were to cease, we should still be faced with fundamentally the same problems which have always faced us. Secondly, I assert that conspiracies are very rarely successful. The results achieved differ widely, as a rule, from the results aimed at. ...

We see here clearly that not all consequences of our actions are intended consequences; accordingly, that the conspiracy theory of society cannot be true because it amounts to the assertion that all events, even those which at first sight do not seem to be intended by anybody, are the intended results of the actions of people who are interested in these results. (Popper, 341-2)

Popper conceded the existence of true conspiracies; however, his conceptualization of society prohibited giving them an undue amount of influence. Using this perspective one might say, expanding on Pipes example earlier, that if Nazism had not arisen in the 1930s, some other nationalistic, xenophobic movement would have probably evolved in post-war Germany.

Perhaps the most predominant piece of research concerning the influence of conspiracy theories on culture was Richard Hofstadter's essay entitled <u>The Paranoid Style in American Politics</u>. Originally delivered as a lecture in 1962, this short work has virtually monopolized the study of Conspiracism, or the "paranoid style" as he termed it, and culture. Every study of any length mentioned in this review extensively, save the two above which preceded it. Although Hofstadter made a very compelling argument, this singular prominence of a particular work hardly encourages an environment of dynamic research in an already sparse field. This is not to take away any acclaim from the work itself: rather, it is an observation that research in this area has not progressed much over the past thirty years.

Moreover Hofstadter, or more specifically many individuals who have sought to interpret him, fell into many of the same stereotypes afflicting other theorists, such as viewing Conspiracism primarily as a movement of the uneducated, or the politically conservative. Hofstadter himself wrote that conspiracy, "is not a style of mind confined to the right wing" (Hofstadter, xi).

Hofstadter began his investigation with a very basic definition what constituted a conspiratorial frame of mind. He defined it as an essential worldview where:

> The model on which the world is interpreted contains the same exaggeration, the same crusading mentality, the same sense that all of our ills can be traced to a single center and hence can be eliminated by some kind of final act of victory over the evil source. If the warnings of those who diagnose the central treachery are not heeded soon enough, it is argued, we are finished: the world confronts an apocalypse

of a sort prefigured in the Book of Revelation. (Hofstadter, xii)

Building on this foundation, he began to frame more specific assertions regarding the conspiratorial mind writing that the "paranoid style [includes] qualities of heated exaggeration, suspiciousness, and conspiratorial fantasy. ... It is the paranoid modes of expression by more or less normal people that makes the phenomenon significant. The feeling of persecution is central, and it is indeed systematized in grandiose themes of conspiracy" (Hofstadter, 3-4).

Even at his time, Hofstadter recognized that Conspiracism, as a worldview, was not so distressing as the fact that otherwise ordinary people often articulate these ideas. This was a symptom of a larger lack of discernment among segments of the American public. However, he also recognized that the essential connection of conspiracy theories with many historical American movements:

> A distorted style is a possible signal that may alert us to a distorted judgement ... What interests me here is the possibility of using political rhetoric to get at political pathology. One of the most impressive facts about the paranoid style ... is that it represents an old and recurrent mode of expression in our public life which has frequently been linked with movements of suspicions discontent and whose content remains much the same even when it is adopted by men of distinctly different purposes. While it comes in waves of different intensity, it appears to be all but ineradicable. ... In America it

has been the preferred style of minority movements. (Hofstadter, 6-7)

He later continued,

[In the 19th century] the spokesmen of those earlier movements felt that they stood for causes and personal types that were still in possession of their country – that they were fending off threats to a still well-established way of life in which they played an important part. But the modern right wing … feels dispossessed: America has been largely taken away from them and their kind, though they are determined to try to repossess it and to prevent the final destructive act of subversion. The old American virtues have already been eaten away by cosmopolitans and intellectuals; the old competitive capitalism has been destroyed by treasonous plots, having as their most powerful agents not merely outsiders and foreigners but major statesmen seated at the very centers of American power. Their predecessors discovered foreign conspiracies; the modern radical right finds that conspiracy also embraces betrayal at home. (Hofstadter, 23-4)

Hofstadter recognized the historical contexts of these beliefs, but also noted their greater presence in the mainstream. As subsequent studies would mention, Hofstadter also maintained that technology was a key element in the diffusion and increasing scope of conspiracy theories:

Important changes may be traced to the effects of the mass media. The villains of the modern right are much more vivid than those of their paranoid predecessors, much better known to the public; the contemporary literature of the paranoid style is by the same token richer and more circumstantial in personal description and personal invective. ... The theater of action is now the entire world ... in the end the real mystery, for one who reads the primary works of paranoid scholarship, is not how the United States has been brought to its present dangerous position, but how it has managed to survive at all. (Hofstadter, 24-5)

Having placed conspiracy ideas in their historical and contemporaneous context, Hofstadter proceeded to make some statements describing the basic rhetorical style of conspiracy theory:

> The central image is that of a vast and sinister conspiracy, a gigantic and yet subtle machinery of influence set in motion to undermine and destroy a way of life. One may object that there are conspiratorial acts in history, and there is nothing paranoid about taking note of them. … The distinguishing thing about the paranoid style is not that its exponents see conspiracies or plots here and there in history, but that they regard a "vast" or "gigantic" conspiracy as the motive force in historical events. History is a conspiracy,

set in motion by demonic forces of almost transcendent power, and what is felt to be needed to defeat it is not the usual methods of political give-and-take, but an all-out crusade. The paranoid spokesman sees the fate of this conspiracy in apocalyptic terms – he traffics in the birth and death of whole worlds, whole political orders, whole systems of human values. ... Time is forever running out. ... The apocalypticism of the paranoid style runs dangerously near to hopeless permission but usually stops short of it.

Describing the personality types and attitudes tending to follow these ideas, he continued:

As a member of the avant-garde who is capable of perceiving the conspiracy before it is fully obvious to an as yet unaroused public, the paranoid is a militant leader. He does not see social conflict as something to be mediated and compromised, in the manner of the working politician. Since what is at stake is always a conflict between absolute good and absolute evil, the quality needed is not willingness to compromise but the will to fight things out to a finish. Nothing but complete victory will do. ... This demand for unqualified victories leads to the formulation of hopelessly demanding and unrealistic goals, and since these goals are not even remotely attainable,

> failure constantly heightens the
> paranoid   frustration.
> (Hofstadter, 30-1)

The absolute demands of Conspiracism, contrasted with the limited possibilities of satisfactory outcomes, Hofstadter envisioned the paranoid state of mind as a self-fulfilling prophecy incapable of resolution. Once again, this demonstrated that Conspiracism is not so concerned with the pursuit of truth as it is with advocating a worldview.

Finally, Hofstadter observed the types of rhetorical methodology used by conspiracy theorists to state their case.

> This enemy is clearly delineated, he is a perfect model of malice, a kind of amoral superman: sinister, ubiquitous, powerful, cruel, sensual, luxury-loving. … The paranoid's interpretation of history is in this sense distinctly

personal: decisive events are not taken as part of the stream of history, but as the consequences of someone's will. ... One of the impressive things about paranoid literature is precisely the elaborate concern with demonstration it almost invariably shows. ... The very fantastic character of its conclusions leads to heroic strivings for "evidence" to prove that the unbelievable is the only thing that can be believed. ... The typical procedure of the higher paranoid scholarship is to start with ... defensible assumptions and with a careful accumulation of facts, or at least what appear to be facts, and to marshal these facts toward an overwhelming "proof" of the particular conspiracy that is to be established. ... The paranoid mentality is far more coherent than the real world, since it leaves no room for mistakes, failures or ambiguities. It is, if not wholly rational, at least intensely rationalistic; it believes that it is up against an enemy who is infallibly rational as he is totally evil, and it seeks to match his imputed total competence with its own, leaving nothing unexplained and comprehending all of reality in one overreaching, consistent theory. It is nothing if not "scholarly" in technique. ... What distinguishes the paranoid style is not, then, the absence of verifiable facts (though it is occasionally true that in his extravagant passion for facts the paranoid occasionally manufacturers them), but rather the curious leap in imagination that is always made at some critical point in the recital of events. (Hofstadter, 35-37)

These enunciated principles are important because they clearly demonstrate that Conspiracism, or the paranoid mentality – to use his terminology - is not the result of a specific political ideology. Rather, conspiracy theories result from an aberrant emotional reaction to dire social conflicts directly effecting, but beyond the control, of Conspiracism's true believers.

While certain sections of the political spectrum have made greater use of conspiracy theories to forward their agendas, he reinforced the consideration that Conspiracism is a social, as opposed to a political, construct (See Also Pinsker, 1). In his concluding remarks, Hofstadter referenced the fact that this mentality is primarily a social phenomenon historically procured by various political agendas in order to gain support from a wider base of the population using fear and paranoia:

> The recurrence of the paranoid style over a long span of time and in different places suggests that a mentality disposed to see the world in the paranoid's way may always be present in some considerable minority of the population. But the fact that movements employing the paranoid style are not constant but come in successive episodic waves suggests that the paranoid disposition is mobilized into action chiefly by social conflicts that involve ultimate schemes of values and that bring fundamental fears and hatreds, rather than negotiable interests, into

political action. Catastrophe or the fear of catastrophe is most likely to elicit the syndrome of paranoid rhetoric. ... The paranoid tendency is aroused by a confrontation of opposed interests which are (or are felt to be) totally irreconcilable, and thus by nature not susceptible to the normal political processes. Feeling that they have no access to political bargaining, or the making of decisions, they find their original conception of the world of power as omnipotent, sinister, and malicious fully confirmed. They see only the consequences of power – and this through distorted lenses – and have little chance to observe its actual machinery. (Hofstadter, 39)

In Hofstadter's estimation, the "paranoid style," or Conspiracism, is primarily rhetoric of the dispossessed. Praying on the anxieties of their audiences, the purveyors of this narrative use fear and manipulation to gain their various goals. After Hofstadter's succinct statement on the role of conspiracy theories in society, most of the following research was essentially confirmatory. While this is a testament to the Hofstadter's scholarly depth and precision, it is also a concern since the inertia in this research field following his writing has been, relative to other advances in the social sciences, considerable.

Writing five years after Hofstadter, Lipset and Raab contended that, "The conspiracy theory is an extension of historical moralism, peculiarly designed to legitimate the closing down of the ideational marketplace – that is, providing a rationale for accomplishing the very thing the conspiracy theory is presumably directed against: the manipulation of the many by the few" (Lipset & Raab, 17). The authors arrived at this conclusion following a brief discussion noting that conspiracy theories tend to be comprehensively global and historical in scope. They noted the irony of conspiratorial thinking in the sense that,

> It is necessary for the conspirators to be secret, but it is also necessary for them to be somehow identifiable. For the personification of evil in history is another essential element of conspiracy theory. The secrecy, which characterizes the manipulators, tends to make them abstract; the personification becomes difficult unless they are made more concrete. As politically effective weapons, many conspiracy theories have floundered on this

contradiction. (Lipset & Raab, 16-17)

This expanded on the assertion that Conspiracism manipulates through fear, indicating the paradox that the perpetrators of alleged conspiracies must be simultaneously secret, and yet exposed.

Portraying the a dualistic model often associated with American politics in general, and among conspiracy theorist in particular, Davis took a slightly more sympathetic view:

Alarmists have portrayed each subversive force as posing an unprecedented danger, and have accordingly picture the past as a time of idyllic harmony, it is easy to overlook the continuity in American movements of countersubversion, and the characteristics common to them. ... Certainly we should resist any temptation to conflate all warnings of conspiracy into a single "American paranoid mind." … Most were responding to highly disturbing events; and their perceptions, even when wild distortions of reality, were not necessarily unreasonable interpretations of available information. Collective beliefs in conspiracy have usually embodied or given expression to genuine social conflict. (Davis, xiii-xv)

Lasch was not quite as sympathetic, criticizing the dualistic trends in the United States that have "entered so deeply into popular culture and political debate that very issue, however fleeting or unimportant, presents itself as a matter of life and death (Lasch, 60).

Davis reflected the thinking of Popper, writing that, "throughout our history there has been a striking discrepancy between the pitiful weakness and incompetence of most conspirators and the willingness of many Americans to believe that a powerful monolithic, and virtually infallible organization was about to overthrow the Republic" (Davis, xv; See Also Bidinotto, 1). More recently, Bruce Handy expressed a similar sentiment when addressing the latest recycled version of this conspiracy theory, namely the fear of militia groups that the U.S. government has a secret plan calling for United Nations troops to take over America:

> Now there are a lot of reasons why this scenario is patently ridiculous, not the least among them the fact that no one in his right mind would turn the U.N. to pacify a vast and unruly nation like the U.S., not when

Bosnian Serbs defy U.N. troops as if they were to be taken no more seriously than a force of substitute teachers. However, an even larger problem with this conspiracy theory is that the Federal Government doesn't work nearly well enough to execute it, not on the scale and with the level of secrecy and precision the militias envision. After all, government is run by the same people who once paid $640 for toilet-seat covers, who went ahead with the initial raid on the Branch Davidians even though they knew David Koresch had been forewarned, who couldn't figure out that Aldrich Ames was selling secrets to the Soviet Union even when the $70,000-a-year CIA officer moved into a half-

> million-dollar mansion and began driving to work in a spiffy new Jaguar. While government might seem faceless and all-powerful to outsiders, insiders know it's an organization made up of human beings, with all the incompetence that implies. (Handy, 1)

This single instance reiterated the contention that conspiracy theorists are not interested in the contrary facts brought to bear against their musings, since their theories are viewed to be above the ordinary rules of proof and evidence.

Similarly, Bale enunciated several attributes tending to characterize conspiracy theories:

> In the first place, conspiracy theorists consider the alleged conspirators to be Evil

incarnate. ... Secondly, conspiracy theorists perceive the conspiratorial group as both monolithic and unerring in the pursuit of its goals. ... Thirdly, conspiracy theorists believe that the conspiratorial group is omnipresent, at least within its own sphere of operations. ... Fourthly, the conspiratorial group is viewed by conspiracy theorists as virtually omnipotent. ... Finally, for conspiracy theorists conspiracies are not simply a regular feature of politics whose importance varies in different historical contexts, but rather the motive force of all historical change and development. The conspiratorial group can and does continually alter the course of history, invariably in negative and destructive ways, through conscious planning and intervention. (Bale, 3-4)

Although writing several decades after Popper, Bale reflected the attitude that conspiracy theorists have a general tendency to assign attributes of deity to alleged conspiracies.

While not agreeing on every point with other researchers, Davis did concur in that conspiracy theories "have never been the monopoly of a single social class or ideology, but have been rapidly appropriated by highly diverse groups. ... One way of distinguishing different categories of countersubversion is to look at the sources of real or suspected danger" (Davis, xv-xvii). He also recognized the consistency of Conspiracism in American culture stating that it is "interchangeability of images and metaphors suggests that the phenomenon of countersubversion might be studied as a special language of cultural form, apart from any preconceptions of truth or falsity" (Davis, xv). Unfortunately, Davis did not choose to follow up on this thought, and his work largely reflected ideas already expressed by other authors. Exactly the same statement could be made about a more recent author, Daniel Pipes, whose ideas – other than those mentioned earlier in this section – essential reiterated the writings of earlier authors. This was particularly ironic considering his assertion that distaste for intellectual originality or change was an almost unique aspect of Conspiracism: "Originality, so prized by genuine researchers, is unwelcome in this strange world of pseudoscholars where the prestige of old sources overshadows anything recent" (Pipes, 49).

Fortunately, this malaise does not seem to have infected all of those who study the social implications of conspiracy theories as well. Several pieces of recent research herald a new and encouraging quality in studying the efficacy of Conspiracism as a social narrative. Specifically, within the past several years, researchers have begun to ask more specific questions concerning the influential role of conspiracy theories in the worldviews of average people. Bale described Conspiracism as an intellectual construct of quasi-religious proportions:

> Conspiracy theories help make complex patterns of cause-and-effect in human affairs more comprehensible by means of reductionism and oversimplification. Secondly, they purport to identify the underlying source of misery and injustice in the world, thereby accounting for the current crises and upheavals and explaining why bad things are happening to good people or vide versa. Thirdly, by personifying that source they paradoxically help people to

reaffirm their own potential ability to control the course of future historical developments. After all, if evil conspirators are consciously causing undesirable changes, the implication is that others, perhaps through the adoption of similar techniques, may also consciously intervene to protect a threatened way of life or otherwise alter the historical process. In short, a belief in conspiracy theories helps people to make sense out of a confusing, inhospitable reality, rationalize their present difficulties, and partially assuage their feelings of powerlessness. In this sense, it is no different than any number of religious, social, or political beliefs, and is deserving the same serious study. (Bale, 2)

Similarly, Spark and Knight hoped to open a renewed dialogue in order to determine the why Conspiracism continues to find an audience in what purports to be a sophisticated culture. "While it is clear that there is a 'camp' quality to some of the more baroque theories put forward (e.g., that the British Royal family are drug-runners), this should only indicate more strongly the need for an appreciation of the aesthetics of conspiracy-mongering, and for a scholarly enquiry about the meaning of the pleasures, entertainments, and satisfactions which conspiracy appears to provide to such large numbers of Americans today" (Spark & Knight, 1). They continued:

> We hope ... to map and understand the re-coherences which conspiracy imagines and so extensively deploys. That these re-coherences produce difficulties (the irrational, the

racist, the paranoid, the bizarre, the trivial) is not disputes, but this problem is particularly true for an academy which despite its engagement with the popular continues (as Andrew Ross has argued about 'low' culture) to find difficulty with the apparently un-malleable politics of some elements of popular culture.   ...

Therefore, the aim of our studies must be to resist the characterization of conspiracy as (literally) incredible, but also challenge the presumption of it as innately recidivist. In setting conspiracy within postmodern theory we engage particularly with the contention made by [Fredric] Jameson that such thinking represents an over-determined response to the fragmentation induced by late capitalism – that in trying to see everything, it sees nothing. In fact, its desire to plot connections and to connect plots indicates precisely the utility of conspiracy in providing a zone for the imagination in which alternative totalities can be constructed and revised out of mass information. ... Examining conspiracy provides a valuable and overlooked means of understanding popular perceptions of the contemporary situation, and the paradigms which the conspiratorial imagination provides pose serious questions about causation, authority and knowledge in the postmodern globalising era. ... The new prevalence of conspiracy theory and the methodology by which raw information by which raw information is processed and becomes legitimated as knowledge ought to form the basis for study to come, but, as a symptomatic feature of the contemporary condition, the very popularity of conspiracy clearly also figures a postmodern collapse of distinctions between the literal and the metaphorical, the factual and the fictional, the paranoid and the persecuted, the diagnosis and the symptom, the personal and the political, the trivial and the worthwhile, the plausible and the incredible. The loss of these distinctions has served to disable traditional outlooks and politics (including cultural politics), and so the issue of where this leaves the American nation, and whether differentiation between conspiracy as legitimate revelation or deluded mystification is possible and desirable is a project we consider should engage cultural criticism in the future. (Spark & Knight, 2-5)

What these two British scholars have proposed, in view of the apparent failure of traditional intellectual constructs in the face of modern and post-modern society is that Conspiracism may be an effective rhetorical model through which to reconstruct various modes of information collation. Their context does not seem to indicate that this is necessarily the most ideal method, but the construct of conspiracy, particularly in light of Bale's statements, has proved to be an effective method of simplifying vast complexities.

This literature review has demonstrated that Conspiracism and conspiracy theories have always been a part of American life. Increasingly prominent during eras of social of intellectual conflict and apparently a consistent narrative for society's dispossessed, conspiracy theories provide simple and coherent explanations in an increasingly complex world. These types of theories are not the exclusive domain of any specific social group or ideology, but reflect every strata of society at various times.

While no amount of logic will dissuade true believers' faith in the validity of this type of discourse, the fact that conspiracies have been uncovered at various times in American history has proved to confirm conspiracy theorists in the validity of their narratives. The recent trends toward serious acceptance of these theories by broad sections of the general public have made this an important topic of inquiry for those concerned with social trends. This particularly true in the field of communication, because it has been reasonably demonstrated that technology, and broader avenues of general communication have been instrumental in the recent profusion, and positive reception, of conspiracy theories.

3. <u>METHODOLOGY</u>

This research will attempt to analyze a conspiracy theory using an adaptation of the canons of classical rhetoric, as primarily embodied in Aristotle's <u>Rhetoric</u>. According to Foss, this approach, as a form of rhetorical analysis, has been generally out of favor in the Communication field (Foss, 1996, 27). Labeled Neo-Aristotelian, this critical approach came under criticism due to the <u>Rhetoric</u>'s design as an instructional text. Nevertheless, this approach contains several features that make it an attractive paradigm for the analysis of persuasive appeals. Through systematizing principles of rhetoric and logic in argument preparation, the <u>Rhetoric</u> naturally becomes a standard for measuring persuasive appeal. Therefore, the use of the <u>Rhetoric</u> as a model for evaluation is a legitimate pursuit. In the present context, this exploration will reflect Smith's use of the application of Aristotelian-Toulminian theories of logic in the examination of Hofstadter's hypothesis (Smith, 277).

Aristotle described rhetoric as "the power of discovering what the available means of persuasion are when addressing specific issues" (Aristotle, 1.2). Wichelns, one of the early Neo-Aristotelians', was mainly concerned with the direct affect of a message on an audience (Foss, 1996, 24). Moreover, his primary focus was to use these standards in conjunction with spoken messages. Application of the <u>Rhetoric</u>'s criteria to the text under consideration will accomplish this goal. The larger purpose is to expand this paradigm in application to persuasive appeals generally.

Traditionally, there have been five accepted canons of Aristotelian, or classical, rhetoric: *memory, delivery, style, organization,* and *invention.* The first two canons deal specifically with oral communication and are not relevant to the present study. The examination of *style* will focus on the use of language, and its overall contribution to the communicators' goal of persuasion. Thesis development, metaphor, language use, and expressed ideas seek to create an intended response. Under the canon of *organization,* the examination of potential persuasive power of argument arrangement will take place. Finally, the canon of *invention* will analyze *pathos*, *ethos*, and *logos*, of the conspiracy argument. The *pathos* of appeals will explore what role the stimulation of emotion in an audience plays in a persuasive communication. The appeal of *ethos* seeks to establish the credibility of the communicator and his or her argument. Typical examples of this type of appeal will reference the author's credentials, or other authorities. Consideration of the *logos* or logic of the argument will determine the type of reasoning used in the observed text.

Observed in this context, the stylistic analysis of metaphor in Conspiracism becomes specifically valuable. Lawrence Rosenfeld has observed:

The metaphor is, as Aristotle held, a sign of genius, an emblem of the individual's momentary withdrawal from the world into his mental landscape, even as he retains contact with the sensible world with the thread of a language figure … the mental cohesion of inward and outward signaled by the metaphor is the vehicle by which the mind sustains its vitality and "recreates" those attending the rhetorical moment. (Foss, 1985, 145)

The use of metaphors provides a tremendous source of persuasive strength to conspiracy theories, as well as to other socially anomalous messages – such as religious cults, for example. Combined with the elements of *organization, pathos, ethos,* and *logos,* metaphorical constructs create a rhetorical environment that is dynamically energetic. This energy is the fuel for the persuasive engine, and the primary object of this inquiry.

4. <u>APPLICATION</u>

<u>The Creature from Jekyll Island</u>, by G. Edward Griffin, purports to demonstrate that the Federal Reserve is a banking cartel created by a cabal of banking interests with a secret agenda running contrary to the public interest. Through an extended discussion that includes economic and monetary theory, banking, and history Griffin claimed that the Federal Reserve, working in concert with the International Monetary Fund (IMF) and the World Bank, is an apparatus designed to help create worldwide inflation and debt. The ultimate goal of this cartel is the creation of a socialist one-world government: the New World Order (101, 107-8).[1]

Stylistically, Griffin developed his economic thesis based on five "Natural Laws of Human Behavior in Economics" (592-3). His specific use of the term "natural law" to describe his observations is

---

[1] Interestingly, Griffin is not entirely opposed to a world government per se. See p. 515.

significant. The term "natural law" has existed, at least since the time of Thomas Aquinas, to describe those legal concepts considered universal (Feinberg, 17). Therefore, by using this term, Griffin attempted to invest his observations with the authority of over 700 years of jurisprudence. His laws essentially state that money supplies not based on precious metals, and gauged by a system of honest weights and measures, will cause economic hardship and political disunity to follow inevitably. Following this context, Griffin asserted that the Federal Reserve, the World Bank, and the IMF use the mechanism of foreign aid from industrialized nations to third world nations to weaken them both: the former through the loss of money to unpaid, and the later into a debtor's servitude (130, 109). These actions all serve to forward the plans of the Council on Foreign Relations, described by Griffin as "the hidden government of the United States," and "a front for J.P. Morgan and Company" (110, 273). Their hidden agenda is "the building of world socialism," however Griffin posits that the great obstacle to the accomplishment of this goal is the economic independence of the United States (95, 514-5). Therefore, these duplicitous organizations have the military and economic weakening of the United States as a prime directive (see 516-532). In G. Edward Griffin's world, all treaties, organizations, and prominent persons have ulterior agendas, and nothing happens by accident (130).

Griffin attempted to have metaphor play a prominent role in invigorating his presentation. His hope was to make the story, "as fascinating as any work of fiction could be" (iii). He describes his research as setting "off into the dark forest to do battle with the evil dragon" (i). The title itself is his label for the Federal Reserve: the Creature from Jekyll Island. This imagery recurs in one section title: "What Creature is this?" and two chapter titles: "The Creature Comes to America," and "The Creature

Swallows Congress." Other section and chapter titles included "The New Alchemy," "A Tale of Three Banks," "Time Travel into the Future," "The Secret Science," and "The Best Enemy Money can Buy." However, apart from sectional headings, he did not generally follow through with this sense of imagery within the text. As a result, metaphorical images often seemed disconnected from the substance of the text. They would appear and disappear, almost at random, and did very little to add to the text's cohesion.

Another device Griffin used, specifically in the first and twenty-fifth chapters, was narrative. In each case information was presented in a novella form in order to convey his message with a sense of drama. Both sought to arouse feelings of fear and intrigue to drive their point's home. The former highlighted the meeting that gave birth to "the Creature." It helped set the stage for the exposition that followed. The latter was Griffin's "Pessimistic

Scenario," outlining the United States' final initiation into the New World Order. This section purposely followed George Orwell's <u>1984</u> as a model. Griffin claimed that Orwell's book was a primary archetype for those who sought the destruction of the United States (558). He used this opportunity to summarize and reinforce his main points in a dramatically charged context, and it set the tone for the final chapter that outlined Griffin's solution to the problem of the Federal Reserve.

Organization is a problematic concept in <u>The Creature from Jekyll Island</u>. At the outset, Griffin stated: "Since this is not a textbook, we are not confined to a chronological structure. The subject matter is not a curriculum to be mastered but a mystery to be solved" (1). Even if en written chronologically, Griffin's rambling prose and disjointed structure would make his argument convoluted and hard to follow. The references cited in the earlier stylistic outline of Griffin's theory, attest that important facets of his theory are scattered throughout the text with little appreciation for cohesion. As the review above highlighted, sifting through the text will reveal his basic argument, but only after a great deal of effort. Part of his organizational style is to provide far too much detail to make every point, as well as to indulge tangents of every variety. For instance, several pages speculate about the *real* reason for the Lincoln assassination (390-4). The conspiracy mentioned in this instance had nothing to do with the overall theme of the book, and it did not add anything to the book except for several additional pages of text. With this example in mind, when one is constructing a conspiracy theory, does size matter? Phrased another way, is the structure of The Creature from Jekyll Island a product of editorial incompetence, or is the confusing structure a conscious effort to impress readers with the scope and complexity of the subject matter? Griffin promotes himself as someone who has "a talent for researching difficult topics and presenting them in clear terms that all can understand" (dustcover). The organization of <u>The Creature from Jekyll Island</u> does not support that assertion. In fact, the size, complexity, and disorganization of the text could serve to tax readers' faculties to the point where just about any argument offered by the author might seem reasonable.

According to Aristotle, a communicator should avoid arousing strong emotions in an audience, because their judgment will be warped (Aristotle, 1.1). However, in another place – speaking of the use of fear as a means of persuasion – he stated, "The speaker must bring them into the right frame of mind so that they shall take themselves to be the kind of people who are likely to suffer" (Aristotle, 2.5). Fear is the emotion that encapsulates the pathos of <u>The Creature from Jekyll Island</u>. According to Griffin:

In spite of two incomes, the real net worth of the average household is falling. The amount of leisure time is shrinking. The percentage of Americans who own their home is dropping. The age at which a family acquires a first home is rising. The number of families counted among the middle class is falling. The size of family savings is smaller. The number of people living below the officially defined poverty level is rising. The rate of personal bankruptcy is triple of what it was in the 1960's. Over 90% of all Americans are broke at age 65. (514)

Although the assertions above were provided without any documentation, Griffin also made sure to cite other issues that should concern the average American such as depleted purchasing power, trade deficits, foreign ownership of American property, recession, and the incredible profits reaped by financial institutions from war (20, 145, 230-3, 512). Finally - after implicating currency debasement as a major factor in the fall of the Roman Empire – Griffin wove his theories of the Federal Reserve and the New World Order as the cause for this multitude of woes (22-3, 110-2, 150-1). The dissemination of fear is indispensable to Griffin's persuasive model.

The *ethos* of <u>The Creature from Jekyll Island</u> comes from a variety of sources. Although the Aristotelian standard of *ethos* calls for credibility to be established within the text of an argument, adjacent considerations – such as credentials, or even the purchasing process - may also be influential (Aristotle, 1.2). Griffin's web site (www.realityzone.com) is a fully functional, online storefront. The ordering process is quick and easy. At any given time a customer can know exactly where an order is in the delivery process. Purchases, shipped via United Parcel Service, are Internet monitored from conception to delivery. These peripheral issues of customer service advance the credibility of the author and by extension his text, even before delivery. The book itself, at 608 pages, is physically weighty. One would presume that this would also reflect on the quality of the contents. Likewise, the bibliography of over 180 titles also creates the impression that this is an important work. The dustcover provides a summary of the book, testimonials, and a lengthy exposition on the credentials of the author. These physical features all contribute to the perceptual credibility of the book.

As mentioned earlier, the convoluted structure of <u>The Creature from Jekyll Island</u> added unnecessary intricacy to the point of confusion. This may have been the product of either a conscious editorial decision, or ineptitude. In either case, the additional effort required to outline the facets of

Griffin's theory creates additional steps of complexity in an already complex work. This served to make the book seem more cerebral. The production of such a large and complex work receives an aura of credibility by the sheer act of its creation. Moreover, following the elaborate construction of the book, Griffin's solution to the problem of the Federal Reserve is very simple. Although an act of Congress is all that would be required to end the Federal Reserve system, Griffin proposed a sixteen-point plan to simultaneously return to a gold standard and eradicate the Federal Reserve, with relatively minimal negative repercussions on national economic life. He then encouraged the reader to educate others to reverse current trends through the election of Representatives and Senators. He emphasized expediting this process, inserting rare instance of direct metaphor, and saying:

The Creature has grown large and powerful since its conception on Jekyll Island. It now roams across every continent and compels the masses to serve it, feed it, obey it, worship it. If it is not slain, it will become our eternal lord and master. ... The crusade has already begun. (588)

Finally, there is the *logos* of the argument constructed by Griffin. Aristotle contended that induction, deriving a general concept through the observation of specific cases, is the basis for all reason (Aristotle, 2.20). The fact that this idea is the basis of most scientific methodologies tends to confirm his accuracy on this point.[2] Therefore, one would expect the exhaustive examination of a subject to be inductive in

---

[2] Incidentally, Aristotle preferred deductive reasoning when dealing with an issue rhetorically, but this seems to be a stylistic distinction (Aristotle, 2.20).

nature. This is not the case in <u>The Creature from Jekyll Island</u>. Before examining a single issue, the existence of conspiracy was already perceived as a given. When he finally got around to it, Griffin stated his primary guiding presupposition quite simply: "Conspiracies are the norm, not the exception" (130).

5. CONCLUSION

Conspiracy is in the eye of the beholder. A conspiracy text may follow every "legitimate" rhetorical principle extent, using accurate facts and reasoning. However the key to conspiracy theories is not only in their rhetoric, but also in their presuppositions. The waning influence of traditional mores and myths in modern culture may partially explain the growth of Conspiracism. Karl Popper postulated that the conspiracy theory of society resulted from abandoning God in favor of lesser gods: sinister groups responsible for a multitude of evils (Popper, 123). The conspiracy theorist is a builder of mythos, and has a tendency to take on the office prophet. Even a secular writer such as G. Edward Griffin has seemingly received such a divine anointing:

> I have just finished reading your marvelous book, and must declare that the information

you presented has cleared more sleep from my eyes than any other printed information, with exception to the Holy Bible. And I recognize that the Holy Spirit of GOD is with you in your investigative journey. (Testimonial from the American Media web site: www.realityzone.com)

Hofstadter described conspiracy theories as rhetoric of the dispossessed. In terms of rhetorical style, conspiracy theories tap into the hopes, dreams and aspirations of individuals, especially those who fell they are dispossessed in some way, on a para-religious level. They attempt to do this by taking the chaos of reality and molding it into a systematic structure, albeit often through the highly suspect invocation of fear. Finally, conspiracy theories have one particular stylistic advantage over almost every other type of persuasive communication: neutrality or equivocation is impossible. Moreover, an essential aspect of Conspiracism is the call to action. Due to these factors, conspiracy theories demand decisions, they demand actions, and they demand them *now*.

From the perspectives of communication and rhetoric, this dynamic insistence may be a key factor to explaining the popular interest in conspiracy theories. Very few social, religious, or political movements in history have started without a call to action. However, in the realm of Conspiracism, practically the only requirement from the audience is a response. However, the fact that this dynamism is fueled by such raw emotions as fear, anxiety, and paranoia make an endorsement of this persuasive construct problematic, if not impossible. Through the invocation of these volatile passions, according to Aristotelian theory, the judgment of an audience may be impaired, invalidating the legitimacy of a message. At this point persuasion becomes manipulation, and any "good" proceeding from such a message may be suspect at best. This is a very broad assertion. Confirmation will only be possible through the application of the methodology employed here to a wide variety of conspiracy texts, and a collation and analysis of the collected results. This would form a cohesive basis for an in-depth qualitative analysis of Conspiracism as a social construct.

Finally, in addition to forming an analytical paradigm for the examination of conspiracy theory as a communication form, this research has also demonstrated other important points. First, the tenets and techniques G. Edward Griffin provided a specific case study in conspiracy rhetoric and methodology. The findings of this particular study, combined with the review of earlier literature, tend to indicate where a broader qualitative examination of Conspiracism would probably lead. In addition, through the specific use of a classical methodology, this research has demonstrated that

Aristotelian precepts provide a broad framework for the analysis, and even deconstruction, of persuasive messages. This analytical method will continue as a useful tool, examining the employment of language as a persuasive tool for Conspiracism, as well as in other social messages.

BIBLIOGRAPHY

Aristotle. Lane Cooper, ed. The Rhetoric. Englewood Cliffs: Prentice-Hall, 1932.

Bale Jeffery M. "'Conspiracy Theories' and Clandestine Politics." Summer, 1996. Lobster: Journal of Parapolitics, Intelligence, and State Research. Online. AOL. 01 Nov. 1998. (www.knowledge.co.uk.xxx/lobster/)

Berlet, Chip. "Paranoid Conspiracism and the Right." The Public Eye. Online. AOL. 29 Sept. 1998. (www2.cybercities.com/g/golem/pol phil.html)

Bidinotto, Robert J. "A Powerful Force is Dragging Society Down." Human Events 10 May 1996: 10.

Coughlin, Paul T. Secrets, Plots, and Hidden Agendas. Downers Grove, IL: InterVarsity Press, 1999.

Davis, David Brion. The Fear of Conspiracy. Ithaca: Cornell University Press, 1971.

Feinburg, Joel. Hyman Gross. Philosophy of Law. Belmont, CA: Wadsworth Publishing Company, 1986.

Foss, Sonja K., Karen A. Foss, Robert Trapp. Contemporary Perspectives on Rhetoric. Prospect Heights, IL: Waveland Press, 1985.

Foss, Sonja K. Rhetorical Criticism. Prospect Heights, IL: Waveland Press, 1996.

Goertzel, Tim. "Belief in Conspiracy Theories." Political Psychology Vol. 15, No. 4. (1994): 731-742.

Griffin, G. Edward. The Creature from Jekyll Island. West Lake Village, CA: American Media, 1994.

Handy, Bruce. "A Conspiracy of Dunces." Time 22 May 1995: 82.

Hofstadter, Richard. The Paranoid Style and American Politics. New York: Alfred A. Knopf, 1965.

Jensen, Joli. *Redeeming Modernity*. Newbury Park, CA: Sage, 1990.

Johnson, George. "The Conspiracy That Never Ends." *New York Times*. 30 Apr. 1995, late ed., Sec. 4: 5.

---. "Pierre, Is That a Masonic Flag on the Moon?" *New York Times*. 24 Nov. 1996, late ed., Sec. 4: 4.

Lasch, Christopher. *The Minimal Self: Psychic Survival in Troubled Times*. New York: W.W. Norton, 1984.

Lipset, Seymour Martin, and Earl Raab. *The Politics of Unreason*. New York: Harper & Row Publishers, 1970.

Marin, Rick and T. Trent Gegax. "The Sum of All Our Fears." 31 Dec. 1996. *Newsweek*. Online. AOL. 01 Nov. 1998.

Neumann, Franz. *The Democratic and the Authoritarian State*. Glencoe, IL: The Free Press, 1957.

Pinsker, Sanford. "What We Talk About When We Talk About Paranoia."

Academic Questions. Spring, 1997:
11.

Pipes, Daniel. _Conspiracy_. New York: The
Free Press, 1997.

Popper, Karl. _Conjectures and Refutations_.
New York: Harper Torch Books,
1963.

Ramsay, Robin. "Of Conspiracies and
Conspiracy Theories: The Truth
Buried By the Fantasies." _Political
Notes No. 128_ 20 Apr. 1996.
(www.connect.ie/emc/MEDIA/Cons
piracies/Truth.html)

Ringler, Hugo. "Heart or Reason? What we
don't want from our speakers." _Unser
Wille und Weg_ 7(1937) _Calvin College
German Propaganda Archive_. Online.
AOL. 29 Sept. 1998.
(www.calvin.edu/academic/cas/gpa/r
ingler.htm)

Shils, Edward A. _The Torment of Secrecy_.
Glencoe, IL: The Free Press, 1956.

Smith, Craig Allen. "The Hofstadter
Hypothesis Revisited: The Nature of

Evidence in Politically 'Paranoid' Discourse." <u>The Southern Speech Communication Journal – 42</u>. Spring, 1977: 274-289.

Spark, Alasdair and Peter Knight. "Conspiracy Thinking and Conspiracy Studying." <u>Centre for Conspiracy Culture</u>. Online. AOL. 01 Nov. 1998. (www.wkac.ac.uk/research/ccc/spark ess.htm)

Also Available by Thomas Adamo:

Lex Rex – The Law, The King
A Biblical primer on the purpose, place, and power of
civil government. Samuel Rutherford's *Lex Rex* for the
modern reader.

"The ideas in *Lex Rex* predate modern concepts of
nationalism and politics. They are older than the United
States Constitution, as well as the American Revolution –
where many modern ideas of liberty originated. *Lex Rex*
is even older than the Enlightenment that receives so
much credit for concepts such as popular sovereignty,
limited government, separation of powers, and individual
liberty. Nevertheless, Samuel Rutherford's *Lex Rex* –
written at a time that viewed kings as vessels of divine
power – raised a Scriptural standard arguing for the
dignity of the people and the accountability of earthly
governments. Although some would seek to pigeonhole
the book as merely a tract on civil resistance, *Lex Rex*
contains a comprehensive examination of a Christian
view of civil government. In doing so, *Lex Rex* actually
formulates a blueprint for freedom applicable for any
time and any place. Rutherford hoped to demonstrate
the need for government based on law instead of the
arbitrary decisions of fallible humanity. Throughout this
process, the Bible is the final authority and basis for law.
This Scriptural base was a primary reason for both the
great support and opposition that met *Lex Rex*."
-From the Introduction